Beth Glandfield

D1533532

OUR WORLD IN COLOUR
AUSTRALIA

Beth Glandfield

OUR
WORLD IN
COLOUR
AUSTRALIA

Photography by Dallas and John Heaton
Text by Paul Raffaele

The Guidebook Company Limited

Copyright © 1989, The Guidebook Company
Limited, Hong Kong

All rights reserved, no part of this publication may be
reproduced or transmitted in any form or by any
means, electronic or mechanical, including
photocopy, recording or any information storage and
retrieval system, without permission from the
publisher.

Distributors
Australia and New Zealand: The Book Company,
100 Old Pittwater Road, Brookvale, NSW 2100, Australia.
Canada: Prentice Hall Canada,
1870 Birchmount Road, Scarborough, Ontario MIP 257,
Canada.
Hong Kong: China Guides Distribution Services Ltd.,
14 Ground Floor, Lower Kai Yuen Lane, North Point, Hong Kong.
India and Nepal: UBS Publishers' Distributors Ltd.
5 Ansari Road, Post Box 7015, New Delhi 110 002, India.
Singapore and Malaysia: MPH Distributors (S) PTE Ltd.,
601 Sims Drive, No. 03/07-21, Pan-I Complex, Singapore 1438.
UK: Springfield Books Limited,
Springfield House, Norman Road, Dendy Dale,
Huddersfield HD8 8TH, West Yorkshire, England.
USA: Publishers Group West Inc.,
4065 Hollis, Emeryville, CA 94608, USA.

Text and captions by Paul Raffaele

Photography by Dallas and John Heaton. Additional
photographs by Bill Bachman (24–5 top/lower right);
Roz Forestal (10–11, 40–1 all four, 48–9 both, 50, 51,
52 both, 53 both).

Edited by Lesley Clark and Ralph Kiggell
An A–Z of Fun Facts by Mary Cooch

Designed by Joan Law Design & Photography
Colour separations by Rainbow Graphic Arts Co., Ltd.
Printed in Hong Kong

ISBN: 962-217-081-X

Title spread
*Australia's magnificent Great
Barrier Reef, one of the wonders
of the world, lies just off the
tourist resort of Cairns in
northern Queensland. The reef
is the most extensive reef
system in the world, running
for 2,000 kilometres (1,243
miles). It is also the largest
structure made by living
organisms.*

Right
*One of the most endearing
symbols of Australia, the koala
bear, at the famous Lone Pine
Sanctuary near Brisbane. The
koala lives in high gum trees
such as this, and is found
mostly along the eastern
seaboard. Peaceful and docile,
it obtains its food and drink
from eating eucalyptus leaves.
In some parts of Australia, the
koalas have been wiped out by
deforestation, but the unique
mammal is not under threat.*

Pages 6–7
*Ayers Rock, 3.6 kilometres
(two miles) long and 348 metres
(1,142 feet) high, is the world's
largest rock and a mecca for
many visitors to Australia.
Recently, the rock was handed
back to its traditional owners,
the Aborigines and it is now
known as Uluru, one of their
sacred sites. The rock is famous
for its amazing colour changes
as the sun sets over the
surrounding red-sand desert.*

Pages 8–9
*Most Australians live in the
fertile coastal strip surrounding
the barren continent and have a
passion for water sports like
few other people in the world.
Here, in Perth, competitors take
part in a windsurfing
competition.*

Pages 10–11
*The magnificent Flinders Range
in South Australia. Running
north from the sea for 800
kilometres (497 miles) to
outback salt lakes, the Flinders
offers some of Australia's most
spectacular scenery, and is one
of the best areas for
bushwalking.*

Pages 12–13
*Sydney, one of the world's most
beautiful sea-based cities. Here,
the famous Opera House stands
with the soaring arch of the
Harbour Bridge in the
background. Its multi-arched
roofs represent sails of yachts
seen on the city's harbours each
weekend in their thousands.
Australians are gambling mad
and the Opera House was paid
for by a series of popular
lotteries.*

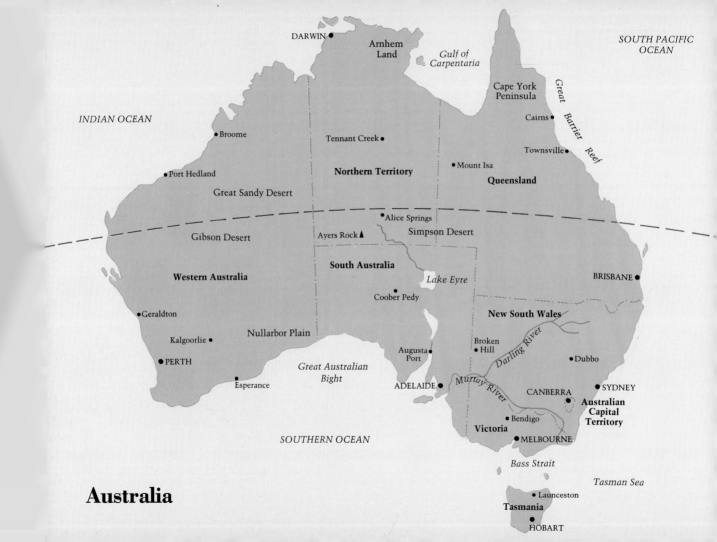

INTRODUCTION

'G'DAY' IS OUR AUSTRALIAN WORD OF GREETING — straight to the point, not a vowel longer than need be, as lean and tough as the stock-men who drive enormous herds of cattle along the edges of the hard Australian desert.

Like the stockmen, under its rough cast it is a word suffused with genuine warmth, friendship and mateship. Being greeted at Sydney airport with a dry 'G'day' from a friend brings tears to the eyes. Not from a rush of patriotism, but by the way that simple word evokes a brother- and sisterhood that bonds all Australians.

Our ancestors faced one of the harshest climates on earth, survived and flourished in this land of great terror and great beauty. Wanderers from Asian lands sailed across the dangerous sea gap in cockleshell boats 40,000 years ago. Many were swallowed up by the ocean or consumed by giant crocodiles and sharks, the guardians of the beaches. But on each journey a few survived, planting firm roots in an unpopulated land.

What the first-comers found was the oldest land mass on earth, most of it flattened, scarred and burned to a crisp by millions of years of boiling sun. Many clung to the shoreline, a narrow strip of green: the fertile, cool, rainforest that ran around much of its circumference, alive with strange but tasty animals, birds and plants.

The more hardy scorned the soft living along the coast and trekked inland, seduced by the shimmering horizon. There, they found desert flowing into desert, flowing into desert, for almost the entire length of the land mass, more than 3,000 kilometres (1,864 miles) southwards, onwards to another strip of fertile coastline and another ocean.

True to our origins, we Australians are a people enthralled with wanderlust or 'walkabout'. In a land that seemed larger than life, our Aborigine ancestors fashioned myths populated by giants and monsters. They gave birth to the land, our 'dreamtime'. Our destiny was swayed by their powerful totems — kangaroos and emus, koalas and wombats, that fed their bellies and their dreams. Their wise men divided the land into lines of song, chanted to the throb of didgeridoos and the clap of dance sticks that mapped the vast continent, geographically and genealogically, with a thoroughness a cartographer would envy.

So they lived through the millennia, painting sacred symbols on cave walls, celebrating their good fortune with corroborees, unaware that in another land, far off to the northwest, ghost-skinned scientists and explorers dreamed of discovering their home, the great south land. This land to the south had to exist, if only as a counterweight for the countries of the northern hemisphere.

Soon enough the new wanderers came, in sturdy sailing ships on journeys that lasted years. The most important was a brave English sea captain named James Cook. In 1770, he sailed the *Endeavour* along the east coast, marvelling at the bounteous harbours, the great forests and the golden-sanded beaches.

Cook steered his vessel through one of the wonders of the earth, the Great Barrier Reef, which spans more than 2,000 kilometres (1,243 miles) along the northern coastline, an endless stretch of turquoise waters speckled with the sun's gold. Led by leaping, cavorting dolphins, he traversed its length, amazed by the beauty of its tropical borderline — the white sandy beaches, the coconut palms and the distant deep-green hills.

Sadly, he and his crew saw hardly anything of the treasures the waters veiled — the wonderland of many-hued coral and the hordes of dramatically coloured fish that swim among its spindly subterranean gardens.

Cook's purpose in charting the great south land, pure exploration, was nobility itself. But what resulted from it sullied the golden shores. Seventeen years after Cook had chartered the eastern and northern edges, the English First Fleet, under the

A very rare albino koala bear at the Lone Pine Sanctuary (top). *A pelican at Yellow Waters in the Kakadu National Park, 220 kilometres (137 miles) east of Darwin. This bird is found quite commonly in Australia's outback, living by the sides of rivers and billabongs* (above).

command of Captain Arthur Phillip, set sail for Australia on a mission that would change the land forever. Some would say for the better, others would say for the worse. The truth must lie somewhere between.

On board the First Fleet were 800 convicts and 200 soldiers. Captain Phillip was charged with establishing a new convict settlement in the great south land. Four years earlier, the 13 American colonies had thrown off Mother England's yoke and declared independence. Having lost the American penal settlements as dumps, the English sought a new tip for society's dregs.

And so ten-year-old pick-pockets and 20-year-old sheep stealers and 30-year-old whores and 40-year-old forgers and 50-year-old murderers and 60-year-old robbers were bundled on board His Majesty's sailing ships for the year-long journey south to the new prison colony on the eastern coast of Australia. They were the new seed that would be sown so casually along the shores.

Convict and gaoler together trudged ashore after a long, hard sea journey. Left far behind, for many forever, were families and the cultural and sinful pleasures of London, Manchester and Liverpool.

They were trapped in a land they had never dreamed of; startling animals called kangaroos that were like giant rats, some six feet tall, hopped along at frightening speed. Giant waves bashed against the shores. The sight of bizarre trees at night was terrifying — the eucalyptus, as grey as ghosts, with peeling limbs twisted into the most devilish forms.

So so, unlike England — grazed by docile horses and cattle, the calm seas of the channel, and with its giant, upright, noble oaks and ferns — was this land.

Their frustration over their cruel fate was released in the vicious curl of the lash on a convict's bare back, by cheering on the hangman with extra vigour at a public hanging by the water's edge or by the deliberate extermination of so many of the original inhabitants who watched peacefully as they came ashore.

From these shameful beginnings has sprung the extreme distaste for authority at the heart of our ebullient national character; the rebellious spirit we call 'larrikin'; a hatred of authority and a willingness to flout it at every chance; and a religious belief that one man is as good as another and that the facts of a person's birth give him no right to lord it over anyone else.

'Larrikinism'. A word we cherish and one to be understood if you wish to know us better. Watch our cricketers, our tennis players, our politicians, our artists. They are all larrikins. Hogan expressed the spirit to perfection in the character of Crocodile Dundee — a true-blue, dinki-di larrikin.

The first English settlement was established by Captain Phillip in the lee of a great harbour named after an English noble, Sydney. Ironically, for a settlement built upon the infliction of misery, a more beautiful site could not have been chosen north, south, east or west for thousands of kilometres.

The great sea wanderer and novelist, Joseph Conrad, sailed into hundreds of harbours around the globe but he wrote of Sydney's harbour, 'It is one of the finest, most beautiful, vast and safe bays the sun ever shone upon.'

That description stands unchallenged today. Now one of the world's great cities, Sydney is a metropolis of a hundred different cultures mingled among the shores of our scenic harbour. Ferries and power boats, huge container ships and ocean liners flit around the harbour all day and night, using it as a watery concourse, plaza and thoroughfare.

A huge bridge spans the divide between the city's eastern and northern shores. In the bridge's shadow is the Rocks, a favourite haunt of visitors, where century-old cobble-stoned streets still weave their way between pavements lined with old pubs, warehouses and stores.

Across the water from the Rocks stands the world-famous opera house. Its glittering white roofs, like raised and puffed-out sails, mirror the thousands of yachts that frolic in the harbour each weekend. Like an enormous flock of colourful butterflies, they flit and dart among the many bays and riverways that bore through the sandstone cliffs, some of them pushing inland for many kilometres.

There is nothing more peaceful than sailing along a quiet Sydney waterway: the swish of the briny breaking over the hull, the buzz of the summer cicadas and the cackle of a pair of kookaburras echoing from the dense eucalyptus that almost overhang the water, the cool harbour breeze and the occasional G'day's mumbled across the water from other lotus eaters on their pleasure boats.

Nearby lie dozens of Sydney surf beaches, hectares of white sand and swathes of green-blue waves. Some break gently on the shore, others turbulently end their long journeys across the Pacific Ocean by hurling crisp-fried surfers at the shore like spears.

Small children, their faces painted like warring Indians with multi-coloured zinc cream, scamper in the shallows. Body surfers tangle with the big waves, the experts surging effortlessly towards shore, the novices dumped heavily on the sandy bottom.

Nubile girls wear not much more than their suntan lotion while lifesavers bare their sturdy buttocks, to enable their bottoms to claim a firm grip on the wooden seats of surfboats that rescue swimmers in distress. The sun has a sting in it but all wear their reddened faces and charred bodies with a fierce pride at work the next week.

It is always our custom, our larrikin pleasure, to spend the day of Christ's birth stretched out in the sun on a beach, within sight of Sydney's spiky skyscraper skyline. Bottles of cool, good-tasting Barossa Valley wine on ice from the 'Esky' accompany lunch of fresh salted prawns, lobster and chicken. The only concession we make to our northern ancestry is the cold plum pudding studded with small coins and smothered with custard that follows.

Yet, outsiders have told us that such luxuries highlight a dangerous way of life in the hard times facing the world. Henry Kingsley, the English writer, once noted, 'There is no life for an educated man in Australia: he has only his choice between rowdyism and Lotus eating.'

Too true, Henry. We are a bunch of rowdies, or larrikins, never more in full roar than when we have the traditional enemy, the English cricket team, on the run.

And yes, Henry, we are a people enamoured with leisure, having a good time and damning the consequences. What else would you expect of a people living in an under-populated land abundant with natural resources?

We overflow with the mineral wealth that drives the factories of great industrial powers like Japan. And our vast spaces enable us to cultivate the millions of sheep and cattle that clothe and feed our hardworking neighbours. Our dramatic landscapes attract several million overseas visitors each year, their pockets thick with gratefully received yen, dollars, deutchmarks and pounds. With our easy life-style, 'She'll be right mate' has become our *Mañana* — a seductive wish for a future that goes from glory to glory.

Lotus eating is a way of life in Sydney, blessed with its harbour, beaches and its sub-tropical weather. So too in another great Australian city, Melbourne, 900 kilometres (559 miles) south. It is a subtle city, resembling England in architecture and morality, as Sydney resembles west-coast America. Melbourne was once the financial capital of Australia but as wealth increasingly concentrates in Sydney, it is distinguished mostly by the opening Grand Slam tennis tournament, the Australian Open, held each January; the Melbourne Cup Race in October, when all of Australia comes to a halt for three minutes; some of the most stately city parks in the world; and a nightly parade of fairy penguins on Phillip Island. And last, but by no means least, Australian Rules football, a frenetic combination of Gaelic football, Irish hurling, rugby and a rousing all-in pub fight.

Australian Rules is like an ancient religion, incomprehensible to any but the initiated. Melbourne is the Mecca and a visitor would be foolish to miss the chance to

Taking a characteristic pose is a magnificent great grey kangaroo with its baby joey in pouch. Along with the emu, also found in the millions in the outback, the kangaroo is used on Australia's national symbol.

Australia's favourite folk hero, Ned Kelly. This model is at Glenrowan, where he was captured by police (top). *A citizen of Old Sydney Town, a re-creation of Australia's first city as it was at the turn of the 18th century* (centre). *At Sydney, a re-enactment of the first landing on 26 January 1788* (above).

go to a game. Australian Rules expresses better than any other sport the raw aggression that is both the bane and the delight of our national character. Spend an hour or so in any street-corner pub after dusk and you'll see that for yourself.

Melbourne's three million citizens feel less tainted than Sydney with the convict stain, in this city founded on the Yarra's banks by two squatters in 1835. Sheep-raising was the town's first great industry but that was supplanted in 1860 by the Ballarat Gold Rush, as mad a scramble for easily gained wealth as any in California.

Victoria, the southern state that calls Melbourne its capital, was home to some of Australia's greatest rebels. Many of them were Irishmen who used the wild outback hills as lairs to challenge the harsh yoke of the colonial rulers, the English. They were called bushrangers and we still celebrate them in song and verse, far more proud of these law-breakers than we are of the upright founders of our nation. For a few years, our national anthem was *Waltzing Matilda*, in praise of a nomadic sheep thief, a swagman, who chose death by drowning in a billabong, or pond, rather than capture by the law:

Up jumped the swagman and jumped into the billabong,
You'll never catch me alive says he,
And his song may be heard as you walk along the billabong,
You'll come a Waltzing Matilda with me.

The most famous of our bushrangers was handsome Ned Kelly, a burly Irishman from Euroa, a small Victorian country town, who fought a running battle with the constabulary for years. He wore a strange kind of home-made armour which inspired a famous series of paintings by Sidney Nolan, our most acclaimed painter and well known outside Australia, too.

You can stand on the very spot where poor Ned had his neck stretched by the law in 1880. The old Melbourne Gaol is now a penal museum and the curator will show you the wooden trapdoor through which Ned made his sad journey out of this world. Have a close-up view of his bullet-dented armour and spend a few minutes in a tiny, claustrophobic cell like the one in which Ned spent his last few months.

Mark Twain was right when he commented that 'Australian history is full of surprises and adventures and incongruities and contradictions and incredibilities', but they are all true — our history is full of wonderful characters like Ned Kelly who we revere more than any political hero.

Our history also demonstrates our view that every man should have a fair go in life, we have flung open our doors to the world, to the poor and dispossessed, almost from the days of the First Fleet. The initial wave of immigrants comprised mostly Anglo Saxons and Irish but after the Second World War, the displaced of Europe were offered homes, jobs and a future here. Millions responded and wove their ancient cultures into the national pattern of our life-style. Since the mid-70s, the third wave of migrants has included large numbers of Asians, including almost 100,000 boat people from Vietnam.

Melbourne is one of the most multiracial cities in the world, home to the third-largest concentration of Greeks after Athens and Thessaloniki. You'll never eat a better Napoli pizza than in Carlton and as for Peking Duck, well Chinatown in Little Bourke Street has a dozen restaurants that can serve it for you.

Adelaide, Brisbane, Hobart and Perth — all state capitals — are Melbourne and Sydney in miniature. Each has its own charms but each is essentially Australian, with all the pleasures and vices common to the two giants.

Brisbane is fast becoming a major tourist destination, thanks to the thousands of kilometres of beaches and reefs found along its lengthy coastline. Surfer's Paradise, an hour's drive south, has been transformed by developers into a mini-Hawaii — the Gold Coast, a strip of glorious surf beaches, has become overshadowed by ugly sky-scrapers and engulfed by a tidal wave of Japanese tourists.

To the far north of Brisbane is the Great Barrier Reef, extolled in the tourist brochures as the eighth wonder of the world. This time they do not lie. The Reef, an enormous natural barrier formed over tens of thousands of years by coral, runs to the tip of Australia.

Made up of countless coral platforms, atolls and cays ranging from tens to hundreds of metres in diameter, the reef is separated from the mainland by a channel which grows increasingly narrow as it travels north.

The channel is dotted with over 600 tropical islands, some of them national parks. Tourist resorts, from the most down-market to the most exclusive, have been built on the islands and are launching pads for visitors taking day trips over the Great Barrier Reef, with its dazzling coral and hundreds of species of fish, birds and shellfish.

The Great Barrier Reef is reasonably close, in Australian terms, to the Northern Territory (NT), the haunt of Crocodile Dundee and his mates. Hop in the plane in Brisbane and about three hours later, 2,000 kilometres (1,243 miles) to the northwest, you will find yourself in Darwin, the NT's capital.

Here, the men are tough as chain-mail, drink prodigious quantities of beer daily and, for sport, like to wrestle frisky buffaloes to the ground or go shooting man-eating crocodiles at night. Macho male fantasies seem to grow in proportion to the number of beer bottles strewn on the pub floor at night. And the women know their place; it's back in the steaming kitchen cooking dinner, washing the dishes, changing baby and keeping the fridge stocked with ice cold beer.

The Kakadu National Park, where much of the Crocodile Dundee movies was shot, lies here, and so too does the Outback — a word that we both fear and admire — for it can stun you with its beauty and kill you with its cruelty.

Kakadu, 200 kilometres (125 miles) east of Darwin, has been included on the UNESCO World Heritage List along with such places as the Grand Canyon, the Vatican and the Sphinx. Its jungles and marshlands are home to some of the most awe-inspiring landscapes in the world. Flat-bottomed boat expeditions can be taken along the park's rivers where giant crocodiles will leap up to take hunks of beef, held out over the water on a pole by a guide. Visitors are advised to watch their every step as several careless tourists have been taken by the crocs.

Up here, you will see many Aborigines, many of them full-blooded tribal people whose clans have lived in much the same way for many thousands of years. Their culture is simple yet rich in social, spiritual and artistic traditions.

The Aborigines have a genius for painting, sculpture and dance, while their social structure is rooted firmly in the extended family. Their kinship system is as complicated as any in human history and their egalitarian society totally excludes any notion of individual rulers — a great contrast to the strident individualism that we metropolitan creatures flaunt.

This is a testing time for Australia's inhabitants, original and migrant. It was only in 1967 that Aborigines gained Australian citizenship, giving them the right to vote, freedom of movement and inclusion in the national census. We are now grappling, both in private life and at the most senior level of national government, with the acceptance or denial of guilt for the English invasion two centuries ago and the flowing on of massive compensation to the Aborigines. At the heart of the impasse is the concept of widespread land rights for Aborigines and it will be many years before we achieve a formula that satisfies both sides.

The Red Centre, the very heart of Australia, is 2,000 kilometres (1,243 miles) south of Darwin. The booming town of Alice Springs is the jumping-off point for a visit to Uluru, once known as Ayers Rock, the largest monolith in the world and 600 million years old. Uluru is 500 kilometres (311 miles) from Alice and a bus trip there reveals a landscape like no other on earth.

The desert is coloured blood-red with low sand dunes that flow across the land like small ripples on a pond. Ankle-high saltbush, as tough as steel wool, spreads over

In Queensland, the Tjapukai Dance Group demonstrates the millennia-old Aboriginal way of catching fish with traps. The Aboriginal culture is the oldest known in the world.

Top
In Queensland's world-famous tourist resort, the Gold Coast, a rainbow lorikeet sits, watching the world go by.

Above
With the end of the Vietnamese War, Australia willingly took in more Vietnamese boat people per head of population than any other country. Most settled in Sydney and Melbourne, following their unique culture without hindrance; all part of the new, multicultural Australia.

Right
Kangaroos boxing, a natural way for males to settle arguments in the wild during the mating season. These fights can become so rough that the death of one of the combatants is not uncommon.

the plains. It is a favourite food for the kangaroos who have taken millions of years to adapt to this dry barren land. The sky is like no other anywhere, a dramatic dark blue-purple, naked of any cloud. The immense dry heat hits you in waves, stunning you repeatedly, rather than delivering a clean knock-out blow.

Suddenly up ahead is Uluru, a massive red hunk of rock sacred to the local tribe. It is 355 metres (1,148 feet) high, three and a half kilometres (two miles) long, two and a half kilometres (one and half miles) wide and nine kilometres (five and a half miles) in circumference. Climb it, if you are willing to dare a heart attack, and stand in wonder at its top, surrounded by a vast, bare plain of red sand.

Just before dusk, the tourists gather before the rock's majesty, their cameras set on tripods to catch the extraordinary chameleon performance of sunset over Uluru. In minutes, the monolith changes from ochre to red to orange to blue to violet and then, finally, to a dark shadow in communion with the ghosts of the clans.

There is another ghost that haunts the rock. It was at the untidy tourist camp huddled near Uluru's base that Lindy Chamberlain's baby daughter, Azaria, was said to have been taken by a native dog, a dingo, and never seen again.

Our journey across Australia is almost at an end and finally we come to our national capital, Canberra, stranded in the bush, surrounded by sheep stations and rugged outback. This small city is like a metaphor for our country, an urban settlement wedged uneasily on the edge of a vast wilderness. It expresses much of our national character in close-up. Our profligacy, our need to live in suburbs of free-standing red-roofed houses, each surrounded by a small, sacred plot of ground; our beery rituals of mateship acted out nightly in clubs and pubs.

Crowning the city is the new Parliament House, opened in 1988 at a cost of more than one billion dollars. It is worth a visit, if only to view the lower house, where our politicians hurl abuse at each other in 'debate'.

But to many Australians, Canberra is sterile; it is an artificial city, similar to Brasilia, any heart that might have been developed has been swamped by an obsessive flow of mortar and concrete. To have an individual soul, a city needs to grow organically, haphazardly. It cannot be brought forth by bureaucratic order, as Canberra proves.

Canberra is yet another part of the collage that is Australia, another one of the jigsaw pieces assembled from all over the world. And yet the completed puzzle, the solid picture, is like nowhere else on earth. For that gift of the gods, we Australians call our land 'The Lucky Country', and even though there is a tinge of cynicism in this title, we all believe — the Anglo-Saxon stockbroker and the Vietnamese grocer and the Chinese doctor and the Irish bureaucrat and the Aboriginal rock star and the Italian architect and the Jewish politician and the Arab taxi driver and this Italian–Irish–Scots–Welsh writer — that we live in the best country in the world.

Above
Rainbow lorikeets at the Gold Coast's Currimbin Sanctuary. Australia is home to some of the most beautiful and colourful birds in the world, many of which exist in their millions in the outback.

Left
Yellow Waters Sanctuary at the Kakadu National Park in the Northern Territory. Kakadu is listed on the United Nations World Heritage List and is one of the most spectacular national parks in Australia.

Right
Great grey kangaroo and its baby joey at Anglesea in Victoria. The joey remains in the mother's pouch for many months before it ventures out into the world.

Centre
A belly-heavy pelican takes off at a lake in Kakadu National Park.

Above
Some of the thousands of prehistoric aboriginal rock paintings in Kakadu National Park. Said to be the best in Australia's parks, the paintings are made in traditional X-ray style, showing the turtle's interior.

Top
Australia's best loved bird, the stocky kookaburra seen at Sherbrooke Forest near Melbourne in Victoria. Its call, similar to a laugh, accounts for its nickname — 'the laughing jackass'. The deadly beak is for killing snakes, the kookaburra's favourite food.

Above
A red kangaroo at full stretch in the outback. It moves by hopping on its two massive back legs, its thickly muscled tail providing a counterweight. The biggest 'roos' can cover many metres in a single bound.

The tranquil waters of Bronte Lagoon in the central highlands of Tasmania. The island state, separated from the mainland for millions of years, has an appearance closer to lush Europe than the barren sand deserts of the continent.

A rare relic from the colourful past — a Sydney postbox modelled on those found in England.

Colonial warehouses at Salamanca Place in Hobart, capital of Tasmania. Hobart has not been so eager to toss off its picturesque past as have other Australian capitals. It lovingly retains buildings like these that remind it of its nautical past. Also in Tasmania, Lake St Claire (far left), looking like some scene from the world as it was a million years ago. The rugged beauty of Tasmania's lakes attracts nature lovers from around the world. Tasmanians, as a result, are the most fervent 'greenies' in Australia, with the Green Party gaining state power in a coalition government in 1989.

Top
*Like some kingly robot, Canberra's tele-
communications tower soars over the national capital
from its vantage point on Black Hill. It is as much
hated as it is loved by Canberra residents.*

Above
*The old parliament house at Canberra, in use for
much of this century before it was replaced by a
billion-dollar complex in 1988.*

Canberra was built from scratch in the bush when the two major cities, Sydney and Melbourne, could not agree on which would be the national capital after federation in 1901. Here, downtown Canberra is viewed across an artificial lake, Lake Burley Griffin.

Top
Trail riding in the red heart of Australia. Alice Springs is a favourite destination for overseas visitors who flock to nearby Ayers Rock.

Left
A mural in Alice Springs celebrates the important role of camels in opening up the desert heart of Australia. Brought here with their Afghan riders in the 19th century, they were turned loose when motor transport took over. Now, thousands of camels roam the deserts around Alice Springs, the largest feral herd of camels in the world.

Right
The twin ghost gums, just outside Alice Springs, popularized by one of Australia's greatest painters, the Aborigine Albert Namatjira. He lived nearby at the old German mission of Hermannsburg.

Above
Here, at Sovereign Hill, the olden days are re-created. This small girl enjoys her ride on the 19th-century vehicle. These old mail coaches were essential for communications during the days before cars and planes.

Left
A paddle steamer heads down the Murray River at Mildura in Victoria. Though only the second-longest river in Australia, the Murray is the most important, used by explorers opening up the interior of the country in the 19th century. Trips of a week or more on the converted paddle steamers are popular with tourists.

Right
Hurtling around a bend is the famous Puffing Billy *train in the Dandenongs, on the outskirts of Melbourne. This commuter train now takes tourists on jaunts through the hills at a full 32 kilometres (20 miles) an hour.*

An oddly shaped clump of rocks known as
the Olgas, 32 kilometres (20 miles) west of
Ayers Rock. Mount Olga rises above Ayers
Rock at 546 metres (1,792 feet). To the
Aborigines, the Olgas are the Katajuta,
part of their mythical account of the
world's beginning — Dreamtime.

Gorges cut through the Olgas leading to
cool valleys and peaceful rock pools.

At the top of Ayers Rock, with the Olgas in the distance, a tourist pauses to record his feat, after the exhausting climb (top). Although a desert, the area around Ayers Rock has some of the most beautiful wildflowers to be seen in the world (centre). A signpost at the base of Ayers Rock states that it is 465 kilometres (289 miles) from the nearest town, Alice Springs (above).

Right
The sun setting over Ayers Rock, one of Australia's most endearing symbols. It is a five-hour, nine-kilometre (six-mile) walk around the base.

Left
Two tourists set off on the steep climb to the top of Ayers Rock. The slippery rocks have caused the deaths of dozens of climbers.

Above
Bell Cave at Ayers Rock. The base of the huge rock is honeycombed with caves, all of them deeply significant to the local Aborigines who call the rock Uluru. Seen on the small rock is one of the many Aboriginal rock paintings adorning Uluru.

A fisherman and his son try their luck on the Swan River which fronts Perth, capital of Western Australia. With a population close to 1,000,000, it is a vibrant city, famous for its entrepreneurs like Alan Bond. Although founded in 1829, it only took on real life with the discovery of gold in the 1880s.

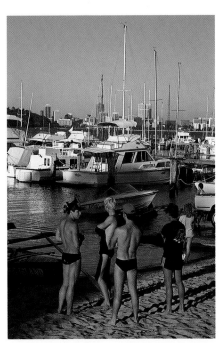

Left
Perth is a place where citizens spend as much time on or near the water as possible. It is blessed with superb beaches.

Below
The Hay Street Mall in downtown Perth, a re-creation of 'ye olden days' England and a popular spot for tourists seeking souvenirs.

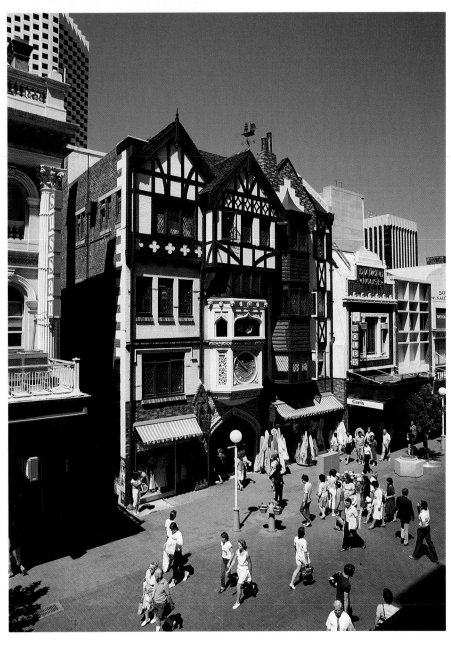

Strangely shaped rocks along a windswept, isolated coastal stretch of South Australia.

Left
Australia was quick to rally to the support of the Empire during both world wars and lost a significant number of its soldiers. Every town honours its war dead with a memorial, although this memorial at Adelaide is particularly impressive.

Above
The most English of all Australian cities is Adelaide which sits on the tranquil Torrens River. Known as the city of churches, Adelaide's other claim to fame is its superb Arts Festival which is held every two years and attracts artists of world fame with its 300 or more performances.

Above
Crowning the Adelaide Arcade is a relief carrying the arms of Australia, an emu and a kangaroo supporting an emblem reading 'Advance Australia'.

Right
Despite its reputation as a 'wowser' city, Adelaide has its bright lights, seen here in Hindley Street with its discos, shops, restaurants and nightclubs, all pulsating with life.

The Barossa Valley, 50 kilometres (31 miles) from Adelaide, is home to some of the world's best vineyards. The 40-kilometre- (25-mile-) long valley turns out about a quarter of Australia's wine from nearly 40 vineyards. The area was settled by German immigrants in the 19th century fleeing religious persecution. The Vintage Festival takes place in March–April in odd-numbered years.

Following pages
The ghostly sand dunes of the Eyre National Park in South Australia, site of spectacular coastal scenery. Close by are some of Australia's best beaches. Various scenes for the movie Jaws *were shot in the Eyre Peninsula.*

Above
Resting in a roadside bay near Darwin is a road train, three massive trailers pulled by a truck. Although these trains are not permitted in or near southern cities, because of their immense size, they are common sights along the long straight road of the outback, hauling loads of 60 tonnes or more.

Right
Some eucalyptus trees are hundreds of years old, their ancient boughs reaching great heights, and their trunks huge girths. Like Australia's curious animals, gum trees have their quirks too: they shed their bark, rather than their leaves; and young leaves differ in shape to mature ones.

Australia is equally beautiful both inland and along the coast. Gum trees provide shade to a cool green carpet of vegetation (top); two fat baobab trees intertwine (left); porpoises sport in shoals along the South coast (right).

Above
The beach seems to stretch forever along the Otways coastline in Victoria.

Left
Surf life-savers rescue swimmers in a demonstration at a surf carnival. Australia is blessed with a magnificent coastline but much of the water is rough surf and so there is a very strong network of surf life-savers who man the beaches to rescue swimmers in distress.

Above
At Anglesea beach in Victoria, a young boy strikes a confident pose, reflecting the mood of this young country.

Centre
Surf life-savers man the reels at a carnival, demonstrating their methods; the lines are attached to life-savers who brave high, dangerous seas to rescue swimmers.

Above
Life-savers wearing distinctive beanie hats, the colours representing their individual clubs.

Left
Australian beaches are not only famous for the life-savers. People there believe they have more pretty girls per square metre of sand than practically anywhere else.

A moment of madness at Melbourne's Moomba Festival, one of the few times of the year when the normally staid Melburnians let their hair down and have fun.

Top and above
A Melbourne tram travels down Swanston Street in the middle of the city. Melburnians really love these wonderful old claptraps. The trams have been in service for decades but, unlike Sydney, any suggestion that Melbourne banish its trams is always howled down.

Left
A clown entertains passersby in the Bourke Street Mall, closed off to all traffic but trams. Here, some of the city's best stores are located including the giant department store Myers.

Melburnians are mad about their football, known as Australian Rules and played in no other country in the world. Here, typically garbed Hawthorn Hawk's fans settle in for a day of cheering their team at the local football ground (top). A programme seller at a Melbourne football game, featuring the Hawthorn Hawks and the North Melbourne Kangaroos (above).

Right
Fans at a one-day cricket match between Australia and the West Indies at the MCG, the Melbourne Cricket Ground, capable of holding over 100,000 people. This was the main stadium for the 1956 Olympic Games.

Above
Hang-gliding over Melbourne during the annual Moomba Festival.

Left
Although Australia is known as one of the hottest continents on the planet, it also has some very fine ski resorts, including this one at Mount Hotham in Victoria. The seasons in Australia are the reverse of those in the northern hemisphere, so many ski fans come out to Australia for their favourite sport at a time when Europe is sweltering.

Right
A parachutist makes a spectacular descent over Melbourne during the Moomba Festival.

Above
*A rowing eight toils along Melbourne's
Yarra River.*

Above
The fair city of Melbourne by the banks of the Yarra. It is a city of parks and gardens, blessed with a more relaxed attitude to life than its rival, Sydney. Sydneysiders, with their beautiful harbour, deride the muddy Yarra, saying it is the only river in the world that floats upside down.

Right
Melbourne's historic Como House, reflecting the English colonial past that has shaped modern Australia.

Above
At Sovereign Hill, a re-creation of a late 19th-century goldmining town, horses provide the main transportation, much as they did when the great gold rushes brought would-be goldminers from all over the world eager to test their luck and strike it rich. Too few did but the gold rush helped settle this fertile stretch of Australian coastline.

Left
Panning for gold at Sovereign Hill.

Above
Tjapukai Dance Group strikes a fearsome pose as they move to the throbbing rhythm of the didgeridoo, the oldest musical instrument known to man.

Right
A mother and child try their luck at panning for gold in Sovereign Hill.

Sydney views
Sunset over the Sydney Opera House (top left). *Sydney's Centrepoint Tower, atop a major city shopping mall, reflected in the glass of a skyscraper* (left). *Sydney's Circular Quay with the Opera House in the foreground of modern skyscrapers. Sydney, more than most, is a city that lives on the water. A ferry passes by the Opera House, on its way to the harbourside Taronga Park Zoo. This is the very spot where the British set up their first colony in Australia on 26 January 1788* (above).

Above
A young girl dressed in a colonial costume feeds a goat at Old Sydney Town, a recreation of life when the British first settled here. Goats were introduced by the British and are now regarded as serious pests in Australia. They are responsible for the extinction of smaller mammals who cannot compete with them for food sources in the wild.

Left
A cottage in Old Sydney Town. The original buildings were made of sandstone, found in great quantities around Sydney's foreshores.

Above
At Old Sydney Town, two tourists ride in a bullock train, a common form of transportation in the early days of the colony.

Right
The bullock master checks the yoke on his cart before setting out on another journey. In the old days, the bullock trains travelled all over the country. They remain only at Old Sydney Town and other re-creations of Australia's colourful past.

Following pages
The Three Sisters at Katoomba, on Sydney's outskirts. The Blue Mountains were a serious barrier to expansion out from early Sydney. It was not until 1813, years after the colony was founded, that a way was discovered through the imposing mountains. The blue haze that gives the mountains their name comes from eucalyptus oil. The Blue Mountains are the favourite place for Sydney's bushwalkers.

Above
Surf life-savers crash through the waves in their boat at a Bondi carnival.

Right
A board rider heads out into the surf along the Gold Coast, a popular tourist resort set amid a stretch of golden beaches, about an hour's drive from Brisbane.

Right
The breakers crash over the shore in a spectacular show at Sydney's famous Bondi Beach. Australians are sun worshippers; each weekend thousands of Sydneysiders flock to the beach, to swim, and relax in the boiling sun.

Above
A typical bronzed Aussie, a surf life-saver at a carnival at Sydney's Bondi Beach.

Right
Up north along the Great Barrier Reef, as well as beaches populated with thousands of sun seekers, you can find coral isles, long stretches of water and golden beaches where you might see just one person in a month.

Above
The fabled surf of Queensland's Gold Coast. Four decades ago it was barely populated, but now tourists from around the world flock to this 35-kilometre (22-mile) stretch of beaches, to swim and soak up its generous daily dollops of sunshine.

Left
Australia's largest northern city, Brisbane, set on a loop of the Brisbane River. The city has a subtropical climate, reflected in its easy-going life style and suburban houses set on stilts to catch the river breezes. As with most Australian coastal cities, its people spend much of their time on the water swimming or sailing.

Right
A surfer heads off to the beach along the Gold Coast. The streets are lined with garish skyscrapers but the beaches are some of the best in the world.

Following pages
Sydney at sunset.

Page 80
Bondi life-savers set out to challenge the waves, practising saving surfers from the breakers.

AN A TO Z OF FUN FACTS

A

Aborigines The Aboriginal culture is the oldest known in the world. They have lived on the Australian continent for an estimated 40,000 years and can stand all extremes of climate there. When the first white settlers arrived in the late 18th century, there were an estimated 300,000 Aborigines in Australia. Today, there are some 200,000 — about 1.5% of the population.

Adelaide Established in 1836. No convicts were ever shipped to Adelaide. The city's growth was financed by real estate speculation and copper mining. Adelaide is known for its Arts Festival, held in March every year.

Air travel 33 international airlines fly into Australia. The four major international airports are at Sydney, Melbourne, Perth and Brisbane. Two major domestic airlines, Australian Airlines and Ansett, fly to all major cities.

Alice Springs (NT) Founded in 1872. Originally it was a repeater station on the Overland Telegraph Line which linked Australia with the rest of the world. It is almost at the geographical centre of Australia, situated in the MacDonnell Ranges. Today, the town caters for tourists visiting central Australia, especially Ayers Rock and the Olgas.

Alligator River A misnamed river in the Northern Territory which is full of crocodiles. The crocodile is common in Northern Australia and people are advised not to swim in rivers because of them.

Amber nectar One of the many Australian expressions for beer.

Anzac Day National annual holiday on 26 April which commemorates the ill-fated landing of Australian and New Zealand troops at Gallipoli in 1915.

Area 7,686,850 km² (2,967,909 mi²).

Aussie Rules The Australian version of football which seems to have no rules at all.

Australia Day National annual holiday on 26 January which celebrates the arrival of the first convict ships at Sydney in 1788.

Australian Capital Territory (ACT) An area approximately 2,400 km (926 mi) on the east side of the continent. It is surrounded by the state of New South Wales. The capital of Australia, Canberra, is located in Australian Capital Territory.

Ayers Rock Situated in the Northern Territory, Ayers Rock is over 300 m (1,000 ft) high and more than 12 km (seven and a half miles) around the base. The Aborigines call it Uluru and it is a sacred site to them. In 1985, the Australian Government gave ownership of Ayers Rock to an Aboriginal trust. The trust then leased it back to the government as a national park. The official celebrations for this arrangement were not attended by the Aborigines. Instead they sent a note to Bob Hawke, the Prime Minister. It read 'Dear Bob, Have gone bush for law business and celebration. Please put "title papers" under the door of our office. Thank you. The Mutitjulu Community (on behalf of the traditional owners).'

B

Banana bender Rhyming slang for Queenslander.

Bark paintings Aboriginal paintings which also serve as maps to the initiated Aborigines.

Bass Strait The strip of sea which separates Tasmania from Australia. It was 'discovered' by George Bass and Matthew Flinders in 1798.

Blue Mountains (NSW) Part of the Great Dividing Range. The Blue Mountains lie west of Sydney and from a distance shimmer blue from eucalyptus oil.

Botany Bay Site of the landing of the first convict ships in 1788. Originally called Stingray Bay, the name was changed to Botany Bay because of the profusion of plant life.

Brisbane The state capital of Queensland, located in the southeastern corner of the state.

Broken Hill An outback region of New South Wales where the oldest human remains were found at Lake Mungo. The lake dried up 10,000 years ago. Kitchen waste found near the lake is estimated to be 38,000 years old. Evidence of a cremation has also been found, estimated to have been carried out 30,000 years ago.

Broome (WA) This small town was the capital of the world's pearl fishing industry in the 1920s. On the coastline nearby, giant dinosaur tracks can be seen imprinted in the rocks when the tide goes out. The footprints are believed to be 130 million years old.

Bungle Bungles (WA) A range of ancient mountains in the remote northwestern area of Australia.

C

Canberra Also known as the Bush Capital. Capital of Australian Capital Territory and of the whole of Australia. Canberra is the home of the Houses of Parliament, the Governor-General and many politicians. Both Sydney and Melbourne were rivals for the title of capital, so Canberra was built as a compromise. In 1911 an international competition was held for a city plan. It was won by an American, Walter Burley Griffin. His plan included the layout of the city and a large artificial lake which bears his name. A spectacular new Parliament Building has recently been completed. Canberra now has a population of 250,000 people.

Climate Australia's climate has tremendous variations, from tropical in the north to mild and temperate in the south. Many parts are prone to flooding in the wet season and to drought and fire in the dry season. Some mountain areas have sufficient snowfalls for skiing.

Cook, Captain James The English explorer who landed on the previously 'unknown' east coast in April 1770. He missed what is now Sydney Harbour, sailing past it in the belief that it was only a small inlet. Back home, the government of the day was not impressed with Cook's discovery, believing it to be a barren and inhospitable land.

Corroborees Aboriginal ceremony at which songs and dances are performed and stories told and exchanged.

Crocodiles The largest crocodile in the world lives in Northern Australia — the estuarine or saltwater crocodile. The longest estuarine crocodile was shot in 1957 and was 8.52 m (28 ft 4 in) long.

Daintree Rainforest Rainforest in northern Queensland which has been the subject of much debate between the state government and conservationists. The efforts of the 'greenies' have preserved the forest intact.

Darwin (NT) Largest town in the Northern Territory. It was bombed 59 times by the Japanese in the Second World War. In 1974 it was totally flattened by a cyclone. It has since been completely rebuilt.

Dreamtime A phrase coined by a British anthropologist earlier this century. It refers to the Aborigines' mythology which is the basis for their thought and practice.

Ethnic groups 98% of Australians are of European origin. About 2% are of Asian or Aboriginal origin.

Esky Australian word for a portable ice box.

Finke River (NA) A deep, dry river as wide as the Nile which winds through hundreds of miles of desert.

Flinders Range (SA) Ancient mountains in which rocks dating back 1,000 million years have been found. The range is part of the Great Artesian Basin area.

Flinders, Matthew Navigator and explorer who mapped the continent by circumnavigating it in 1802 and 1804.

Government The eight states of Australia were separate governments until the federation was created on 1 January 1901. There are now six separate State and two Territory Governments, five of which have their own Houses of Representatives. There is also a Federal Parliament which is based in Canberra.

Great Artesian Basin Massive underground source of water in southern Australia. It is tapped by a series of bores.

Great Barrier Reef The largest coral reef in the world, 2,028 km (1,260 mi) long, situated off the coast of Queensland.

Great Dividing Range Mountain range running parallel with the east coast for more than 2,000 km (1,250 mi).

Greenies The Australian word for the Greens or conservationists.

Highest point Mount Kosciusko 2,228 m (7,300 ft) high — part of Great Dividing Range.

Jenolan Caves Situated in New South Wales, these caves are famous for the stalactite and stalagmite formations.

Joey A baby kangaroo.

Kangaroo Also known as macropods or hopping marsupials. The largest kangaroos are the red kangaroos — an adult male can stand as tall as seven feet. The highest recorded hopping speed of a kangaroo is 64 km/h (40 mph). The highest recorded jump is 3.1 m (10 ft).

L

Lake Eyre Largest salt lake and lowest point of continent at 15 m (50 ft) below sea level.

Location Australia is located between the Indian and South Pacific Oceans on the Tropic of Capricorn. Australia's land mass accounts for one quarter of the entire Asian-Pacific region, but contains only 0.5% of the population.

M

Marble Bar Located in West Australia, where the remains of the oldest organisms, believed to be 3,500 million years old were discovered.

Melbourne Situated in Victoria, Melbourne was established in 1837. It now has the third largest Greek population of anywhere in the world including Greece. Amongst other things, Melbourne is famous for the national horse race, the Melbourne Cup, held on the first Tuesday of November, which is a local holiday for the occasion.

N

Namatjira, Albert Aboriginal artist, who is one of Australia's most famous painters.

Nullarbor Plain (SA/WA) Vast area of limestone on which trees are unable to grow ('nullabor' is latin for no trees). Beneath the limestone are underground streams and huge caves.

O

Official name Australia's official name is the Commonwealth of Australia.

Olgas, The Situated 32 km (20 mi) from Ayers Rock in Central Australia, the Olgas are a group of 28 boulders, called Katatjuta (place of many domes) by the Aborigines.

Outback Australian term for the rural areas.

P

Perth Located in Western Australia, Perth is the world's remotest city.

Pinnacles Desert A desert in Western Australia famous for its standing stones. The site of the pinnacles was originally a huge sand dune, stabilized by vegetation. The pinnacles were formed, over a few million years, by sand gradually blowing away leaving columns of sand held by the ancient root systems. The sand columns hardened into solid cores of rock.

Population Australia's population is 16.5 million and the population density is $2/km^2$ ($5.2/mi^2$). Despite such a small population on such a huge continent, Australia is the most heavily urbanized country in the world, with 99% of the population living in cities.

R

Religions Anglican 28%; Roman Catholic 26%; other Protestant 25%; others 21%.

Royal Flying Doctor Service One of Australia's most famous institutions, it provides the medical attention for the Outback.

S

Snakes Australia is home to a number of snakes, the most venemous being the Sea Snake (*hydrophis belcheri*) which is found at Ashmore Reef in the Timor Sea in northwest Australia. The most venemous land snake is the Smooth Scaled Snake (*parademansia microlepidotus*) found in Queensland and western New South Wales.

Snowy Mountains (NSW) Mountains in the south of New South Wales, known for skiing.

Sydney Founded with the arrival of the first convicts in 1788. Now a large cosmopolitan city with a population of 3.39 million.

Sydney Opera House Most famous Sydney landmark. Designed in 1957 by the Danish architect Jørn Utzon who resigned from the project in 1966 in protest at government interference.

T

Tasmania Discovered in 1642 by Abel Tasman who called it Van Dieman's Land. The name was changed to commemorate Tasman. About half the size of England but with a population of only 500,000, Tasmania has a temperate climate and is famous for beautiful wild scenery and unusual sights such as the Myrtle Forest.

V

Visa requirements Visas are required for all visitors (except New Zealand citizens) and are valid for a maximum of six months.

W

Wandjina cave paintings Very unusual Aboriginal cave painting, depicting a god/creator figure situated in the Kimberley district, WA.

Wolf Creek Crater (NT) The world's second largest meteorite hole.

Z

Zig Zag Railway Finished in 1869, the Zig Zag Railway is famous for its steep descent of the western side of the Blue Mountains in a zig zag pattern. The railway was abandoned in 1910 in favour of a more modern version, but has been reopened for day excursions.

INDEX

GS/23/01